VOLUME 1

Coffee Chats

RESTORATIVE DEVOTIONS FOR
A BROKEN-TO-BELOVED JOURNEY

BEATITUDES PUBLISHING

Copyright © 2023 by Patricia J. Doucet

All rights reserved.

No portion of this book may be reproduced in any form without written permission from the publisher or author, except as permitted by U.S. copyright law.

Unless otherwise indicated, all Scripture quotations marked NIV are taken from the Holy Bible, New International Version®, NIV®. Copyright © 1973, 1978, 1984, 2011 by Biblica, Inc.™ Used by permission of Zondervan. All rights reserved worldwide. Scripture quotations marked NKJV are taken from the New King James Version®. Copyright © 1982 by Thomas Nelson. Used by permission. All rights reserved. Scripture quotations marked NLT are taken from the *Holy Bible*, New Living Translation, copyright © 1996, 2004, 2015 by Tyndale House Foundation. Used by permission of Tyndale House Publishers, Inc., Carol Stream, Illinois 60188. All rights reserved.

ISBN: 978-1-962581-08-0
ISBN: 978-1-962581-09-7

Cover and Interior Design by Ruth Hovsepian
Portraits by Johanna

To You, My Reader

You may have woken up one morning and questioned the value of continuing to live. Perhaps you have cried yourself to sleep more times than you can count. Maybe you have looked in the mirror to see a woman who looked much older than her years. You may have *even* felt God loved you less because of your mistakes, misjudgments, and missteps.

I pray you will find your way to accepting God's incredible love for you. God loves you in your brokenness and desires to restore hope, peace, and purpose to your life's path.

I recently received an inspiring email from a friend who motivated me to continue supporting and encouraging you on your journey. *I am sharing it with you here.*

"I was thinking of people who have encouraged me in my life and you came to mind. You inspired my writing, and a published book was the result. You encouraged my painting, and I love to paint. You encouraged me to take drum lessons, and I begin on Monday evening.

Only a few people are good encouragers, but the gift you have and use has blessed me and many others. I want to say thank you! I encourage you to continue your path."—*Brenda Van Rossum.*

I hope and pray I can also be that kind of friend to you.

30 Inspirational & Humorous Coffee Talk Phrases

Grace Grounds

Latte Laughter

Personal Perks

Joy Jolts

Bible Brews

Exciting Espresso

Coffee Conversations

Mocha Mornings

Bean Believers

Decaf Discoveries

Grounded Girlfriends

Café Compassion

Percolating Prayers

Glorious Grinds

Macchiato Miracles

Mug Mercies

Frappuccino Faith

Roasted Religion
Beverage Blessings
Caffeine Commandments
Java Justification
Inspirational Infusion
Cappuccino Christians
Biblical Baristas
Devotional Drips
Sacred Smoothies
Awesome Arabica
Steamed Scriptures
Gospel Gossip
Warm Worship

—Patricia J. Doucet

COFFEE CHATS

30 RESTORATIVE DEVOTIONS FOR A BROKEN-TO-BELOVED JOURNEY

PATRICIA J DOUCET

Contents

A Note From Patricia	1
1. Cruising for Coffee	4
2. Breaking the Mold	8
3. Struggling With Guilt, Shame, and Worry	11
4. Persisting When the Odds are Against Us	14
5. Rehashing Regrets	17
6. Coloring Outside the Lines	20
7. Navigating Illness	24
8. Appreciating Humor	28
9. Focusing on the Destination	31
10. Getting Back Up After Falling	34
11. Daring to Dream	38
12. Coping with Unfairness	41
13. Enjoying Life	44
14. Staying Rooted and Grounded	47

15.	Lamenting the Past	52
16.	Wanting to Quit and Go Back	56
17.	Pursuing Peace	60
18.	Trusting God's Promises	63
19.	Putting the Pieces Back Together	67
20.	Lighting the Way	71
21.	Hiding No More	75
22.	Re-evaluating Rejection	79
23.	Following the Shepherd	83
24.	Discerning Heart Matters	88
25.	Facing Disappointments	91
26.	Flourishing in the Valleys	94
27.	Believing in Miracles	97
28.	Drawing Close to God	101
29.	Finding Our Way Home	104
30.	Accepting God's Love	108
Jesus Loves Me		112
A Prayer for Salvation		113
Scripture References		116

A NOTE FROM PATRICIA

> "Entreat me not to leave you, Or to turn back from following after you; For wherever you go, I will go; And wherever you lodge I will lodge; Your people shall be my people, And your God, my God. Where you die, I will die, And there will I be buried. The Lord do so to me, and more also if anything but death parts you and me."
> (Ruth 1:16–17 NKJV)

In the Old Testament Book of Ruth, a story unfolds of God intervening in the lives of two women, restoring them from brokenness. The Book of Ruth contains one of the best-loved stories in the Bible—a beautiful redemptive narrative told in four short chapters. It begins with Naomi, her husband, and two sons leaving their homeland in Judah and moving to Moab to escape a famine. Through the years, her sons marry, and sadly, after Naomi's husband

and sons die, she and her daughters-in-law, Ruth and Orpah, become widows.

After these tragic events, Naomi returns to her homeland, and Ruth goes with her. Life was difficult, but God looked after them in ways they could not have foreseen or imagined. Ruth married Boaz, a prosperous relative of her in-laws—providing her and Naomi with a family to care for them. Ruth and Boaz had a baby, bringing more joy than their hearts could have dreamed. It is a story of loss and love, grief and happiness, hope and healing, bitterness and thankfulness, and God's provision, restoration, and blessing.

Let's consider how God can comfort us and gently turn our setbacks into blessings when we offer Him, in prayer, the fractured pieces and remnants of long-lost dreams and aspirations. As we let Him lead us, we will find our way—as Ruth and Naomi did in our Biblical account.

May these daily devotions guide you from a place of *broken* identity to a *beloved* one. Allow them to inspire you to seek God's presence on your journey to wholeness. No matter what adversities come your way, rest assured that God will always be with you, lovingly directing your steps.

"For God so loved the world that he gave his one and only son, that whoever believes in him shall not perish but have eternal life." (John 3:16)

"I will praise you because I am fearfully and wonderfully made; your works are wonderful; I know that full well. My frame was not hidden from you when I was made in the secret place when I was woven together in the depths of the earth. Your eyes saw my unformed body; all the days ordained for me were written in your book before one of them came to be. How precious to me are your thoughts, God! How vast the sum of them! Were I to count them, they would outnumber the grains of sand—when I awake, I am still with you." (Psalm 139:14–18)

"I would rather be a genuine broken person on a journey to wholeness then a fake version of myself, pretending to have arrived."

1

CRUISING FOR COFFEE

"Wait for the Lord; be strong and take heart and wait for the Lord." (Psalm 27:14)

OH NO! HOW WILL I make coffee? It was hurricane season, and although we rarely have hurricanes in our part of the world, we had one in eastern Canada that knocked the power out. Bad timing–I was trekking from the bedroom to my coffee pot for the first java jolt of the morning. Being a coffee enthusiast, I often joked that if I ever had to be revived to save my life, they could hook me up to an IV that pumped coffee into my system, and I'd be wide awake in no time. However, the oncoming panic attack was a different crisis. Brain fog and a mild headache were already making their presence known. I longingly looked at the pot of water waiting to hit those coffee grounds, to fill the house with an enticing aroma. I wondered how long the power would be out as I quickly showered and dressed while aromatic thoughts of hot coffee percolated in my mind. *Time to act,*

I reasoned. As my non-coffee-drinking husband sensed my urgency, he grabbed the car keys, and off we went to see how widespread this electrical outage was. *Would there be a coffee shop that could still brew up a cup of my morning starter fluid?* I looked for other drivers with that glazed-over appearance, assuming they were also looking for coffee. Spotting one, we followed suit–but it was an empty run.

This was not a routine coffee run. After cruising for coffee for about an hour and a half (ninety minutes; people), we found a coffee shop selling the sought-after black gold! We took our place in the drive-thru lineup as my brain fog and headache shifted into high gear. Ah—the aroma gave me hope.

Finally able to clutch and sip my precious morning treasure, we headed home. Upon arriving–before I could place my cup on the kitchen counter, the power returned with its own jolt! *Hmm–if we had stayed home, I would have had coffee at about the same time. But who knew when the electricity would come back on?* With the brain fog and headache now appeased, I curled up on the sofa with my almost empty, warm mug of coffee. *Was the panic cruise worth it?* I reasoned it was. If I had stayed home, there were two factors to consider: the unknown timing factor and the waiting factor. It seemed to have made more sense to do something.

I knew there had to be a lesson here somewhere. Instead of waiting while trusting the power would be on at just the right time, we sometimes take matters into our own hands. We pray, and then, instead of waiting for God's timing, we try to short-circuit the process by tackling the situation on our own, costing us more in many ways than if we had waited and trusted His perfect timing. Stay calm. Be patient. We will get what we need eventually, whether we panic or wait.

We invariably end up with the same outcome while striving and using energy, time, and money when we could have relaxed, knowing things would turn out alright–even if not according to our precise timing.

"Be joyful in hope, patient in affliction, faithful in prayer."
(Romans 12:12)

Prayer

Dear God, help us be patient when we encounter situations out of our control. Whether waiting for the electrical power to return or persevering in a much more significant and severe circumstance, please give us patience and the ability to be at peace while we wait.
In Jesus' name, amen.

COFFEE CHAT NOTES

2

BREAKING THE MOLD

> "The Lord gave another message to Jeremiah. He said, go down to the potter's shop, and I will speak to you there. So, I did as he told me and found the potter working at his wheel. But the jar he was making did not turn out as he hoped, so he crushed it into a lump of clay again and started over."
> (Jeremiah 18:1–6 NLT)

D URING BIBLE TIMES, THE craft of pottery-making was widely practiced. Potters frequently broke apart unfinished work so they could rework it due to perceived flaws.

It is sometimes necessary to break down and start anew for growth. God will allow us to be *broken* at times so He can restore, mend, and heal us from life's hardships, setbacks, and confines, breaking down anything in us that keeps us from fellowshipping with Him.

How does God break down and remold us? In what circumstances would He allow us to be *broken*? Now and again, we get stuck in a mold that restricts us or confines us to a degree. Since God has given each of us free will, our decisions can sometimes lead us down paths that were never intended for us.

Maybe those confines include religious traditions that stifle a vibrant walk with God. Perhaps we have allowed apathy or weariness to keep us from pursuing His best. There may be instances when God allows or causes discomfort in our current situation to capture our attention. He often permits adversities to serve as a catalyst for breaking free from self-imposed or societal limitations. We read about this in many people's lives in the Bible and throughout history.

After this restoration process, and once we desire to take action to grow, the mold gets *broken*, and we are free to discover there is more to the journey than we ever imagined. This process is not grievous, as God loves us, has our best interest at heart, and can see the big picture.

"Yet you, Lord, are our father. We are the clay; you are the potter; we are all the work of your hand." (Isaiah 64:8)

Prayer

Dear God in Heaven, help us submit to Your correction and restoration when we stray or are hindered by thoughts or circumstances contrary to Your will and purpose.
In Jesus' name, amen.

Coffee Chat Notes

3

STRUGGLING WITH GUILT, SHAME, AND WORRY

> "My guilt has overwhelmed me like a burden too heavy to bear. Lord do not forsake me; do not be far from me, my God. Come quickly to help me, my Lord, and my Savior." (Psalm 38:4, 21–22)

"THESE ARE NOT FOR you—they're for the customers!" My father's stern warning stopped me in my tracks! I drew back from where the neatly packed square boxes filled with delicious candy in colors of pink and chocolate peeked through the clear packaging. Ah, Bon Bons—tempting, tasty treats! The car trunk was open while Dad took a break from his deliveries to the candy stores. My opportunity arrived, and with a compelling temptation to snag just one of those morsels of goodness—I decided to risk it! *Surely, Dad won't miss one little candy.* Quick—no one was looking—I carefully extracted a pink one from the bottom of the closest box. *Yay—no one saw me take the candy!* I do not know if Dad noticed that one was missing; if he did, he never mentioned it! I had gotten away with it; however, as delightful as that candy was, it was little reward for my guilt. Alas—I was a thief at only seven years old.

Guilt, shame, and worry are a *toxic trio,* arriving in the depths of our being when something is off. From snatching candy in childhood to fudging the figures on our income tax forms, the dread of facing these three negative emotions is fierce. First comes guilt, shame, and finally, the worry of being found out. In such cases, we can't quite get around or over our sense of self-loathing.

In the quoted Bible verse, the Psalmist, David, laments his guilt and prays for God's help. He addresses God as Lord and Savior, indicating a close relationship with his Creator. When we are weighed down with guilt, shame, and worry, remember that we can come to God through Jesus with repentance, asking for His forgiveness. He will forgive us and not turn us away.

> "Don't worry about anything; instead, pray about everything. Tell God what you need and thank him for all he has done."
> (Philippians 4:6 NLT)

Prayer

Dear God, when we make a mistake or willfully do something wrong, our conscience is troubled because your Holy Spirit prompts us to repent. Dealing with guilt, shame, and worry on our own will not take away the remorse. We ask you to forgive us for trying to deal with these emotions alone. *In Jesus' name, amen.*

Coffee Chat Notes

4

PERSISTING WHEN THE ODDS ARE AGAINST US

"For the Lord watches over the path of the godly, but
the path of the wicked leads to destruction."
(Psalm 1:6 NLT)

I HEARD A STORY about a pilgrim traveling on a narrow path when he encountered an approaching traveler. The oncoming sojourner said in a loud, gruff voice, "I never move out of the way for a fool!" The pilgrim calmly responded as he stepped out of the way—"Go ahead, Sir—I always do!"

When on the road to our desired location, we often meet opposition. Perhaps we are busted and disgusted by detours, discouragement, or distractions because of mistakes or loss of purpose. Our next steps are often not on the beaches of life but on stony paths, steep inclines, and darkened roadways. In some cases, the way forward is dimmed because of flickering light. Yet, God always makes a way where there seems to be no way.

Our attitude plays a large part in our future achievements. To acquire the right attitude, we need the inspiration and clarity to take the next step. With the proper attitude, we can move forward with persistent, steadfast, and unwavering steps, even when the path ahead seems arduous. Encouragement to develop our giftings and talents help. We can make headway with creativity, humor, and generous wisdom from God's Word. Unashamed. Unafraid. Courageous.

A firm grasp of God's Word gives us the strength to continue. Even when we meet with opposition trying to discourage or reroute us, we can take heart because we know the Lord makes a way for us.

"The path of the virtuous leads away from evil; whoever follows that path is safe." (Proverbs 16:17 NLT)

Prayer

Dear God, amid trials and difficult circumstances, help us rely on Your promises to direct our steps and lead us to everlasting life with You. No opposition can overtake us when our assurance and confidence are in You. In Jesus' name, amen.

COFFEE CHAT NOTES

5

REHASHING REGRETS

> "We demolish arguments and every pretension that sets itself up against the knowledge of God, and we take every thought captive to make it obedient to Christ." (2 Corinthians 10:5)

WE REHASH OUR REGRETS as if that can change the decisions we once made. Dealing with regrets may involve realizing we did our best—we did what we could. Yet, we can still be surprised by troublesome triggers showing up when least expected in the form of anxiety, depression, or panic attacks.

We must remind ourselves that when we regret an action or inaction, it is often because we glamorize the outcome had we made a different decision. This is usually because we have information now that we didn't have back then. Forgiving ourselves for failing to do what we wish we had done or didn't do is fundamental to living in peace. Even years after we think we are healed from a regrettable season, along comes a song on the car radio, a movie scene, or the scents we associate with a certain segment of life that can routinely debilitate us. We feel we may have jeopardized a life that might be more acceptable to God or others. An underlying sense of self-abasement creeps in. When we learn to understand what is happening, we can attempt to avoid the triggers and manage our sensitivity to them while being kind to ourselves.

When we offer our deepest and most profound regrets to God with repentance, He forgives and heals us. Attempting to rehash them while trying to understand why we made certain decisions will not help us. *Could-a, would-a, should-a* will only rob us of the gift of the present.

"Godly sorrow brings repentance that leads to salvation and leaves no regret, but worldly sorrow brings death." (2 Corinthians 7:10)

Prayer

Dear God, when our minds recount occasions when we wish we had done something different, let us remember that none of us are without sin. We all stumble in trying to make the right decisions. Please help us be kind to ourselves, knowing we did our best with the information available to us at the time. *In Jesus' name, amen.*

COFFEE CHAT NOTES

6

COLORING OUTSIDE THE LINES

> "Have I not commanded you? Be strong and courageous. Do not be afraid; do not be discouraged, for the Lord your God will be with you wherever you go." (Joshua 1:9)

MY ULTIMATE EUPHORIA AS a child was cracking open a new coloring book—an entire pristine book, untouched, just waiting for me to decorate its pages with color. The scent reminded me of the first day of school when I opened a new four-pack of notebooks. Add a box of forty-eight crayons (with a sharpener), and I was sitting pretty.

I enjoyed the larger box with the crayons arranged in tiered rows. I pretended they were a choir of people, and my imagination led me to put the grey, brown, and black ones in the top rows. Those were the distinguished, tall men with their dark-colored suits. The bottom front rows were all the colors, representing the women in their pretty dresses. A brand-new book meant I had another chance to improve my craft. Mint condition sharp crayons made it easier to stay within the lines. Of course, I aimed to color perfectly—coloring outside the lines correlated with making a mistake.

Compared to *actual life*, coloring outside the lines is often imperative to living well. In most instances, we get to choose the picture or subject, the colors, and how to apply them. While the choices may seem elementary, they are momentous. So, we do our best while attempting to color our life's picture.

I've learned it's often better to color outside the lines than to be bound by them. Genuine creativity typically requires bravery and enthusiasm to see what lies beyond the perimeters of the familiar. We take risks by exploring unfamiliar territory outside societal norms without guarantees of success. Criticism for venturing outside the standard lines or guidelines, whether coloring a picture or in life's decisions, can be discouraging. However, as Christians, we are often called upon to step outside the ordinary, to obey God's instructions to share the gospel. Trusting in God's provision and direction as we step out of the usual into a place of total reliance on Him will assure us of the satisfaction of being and doing our best.

"Each one should test their own actions. Then they can take pride in themselves alone, without comparing themselves to someone else."
(Galatians 6:4)

Prayer

Dear God, help us to take risks and step out of our comfort zones to obey and please You. You promised to be with us as we put our hope, faith, and trust in You. *In Jesus' name, amen.*

COFFEE CHAT NOTES

7

NAVIGATING ILLNESS

> "But he was pierced for our transgressions; he was crushed for our iniquities; the punishment that brought us peace was on him, and by his wounds, we are healed." (Isaiah 53:5)

WHAT'S THAT GRAPE-SIZE LUMP *on my throat?* I pondered this question as I gazed in the mirror while preparing for work as a bank teller one morning. At thirty-five with three children under ten, I was a frazzled wife, mom, business owner, bank employee, and church volunteer, and I didn't have time to think much about the lump. It turned out to be a grim discovery, and a few weeks later, I was diagnosed with thyroid cancer and scheduled for the first of what would be three surgeries.

Just before the final surgery, five years after the first two, I was shaken by the words I heard. The surgeon cupped his hands around my face, saying: "Ma'am, I neglected to tell you this earlier—but when you wake up, you may not have a voice." Say what? He further explained that the vocal cords sometimes get in the way of this extensive, intricate surgery. Upon hearing those words, I was stunned; however, the next thing I remember was waking up post-surgery. With thirty-two carpet staples freshly re-planted in my neck, shoulder, and throat, I was wheeled from the operating room, tears trickling down my face and onto the pillow—again. Nurses, doctors, patients, and visitors walked by my stretcher as the attendant wheeled me down the halls, on and off elevators, and finally, to my room. I felt suspended in time. The noisy trolleys delivered lunch to hungry patients. I was not one of them. The thought of food made me nauseous.

While I was relieved to be out of surgery, panic set in as I remembered the last words I heard before I went under in the operating room. Even though I was still groggy, I heard the words again: *When you wake up, you may not have a voice.* The prospect of never speaking again filled me with a dread that could not be compared to anything I had ever felt. My thoughts were sporadically searching for hope. I prayed to God to let me have my voice. I promised to use it for good in this world. Always afraid of my voice, I was timid about asking questions in school. I frequently hoped someone else in the class would ask the same question I would have asked if not for my insecurities. The thought of losing my timid voice was terrifying. Lying on the stretcher for what seemed like hours, but was likely only a few minutes, I tried to utter a whisper. Then another with a little more force. It wasn't long before I heard my voice, as if for the first time. While faint and weak, my voice was the sweetest and most precious sound my anxious heart had ever heard. This cancer journey was many years ago. I thank God for my recovery and my voice.

We can be inflicted at any time with illnesses, such as cancer or other diseases. We are assured in the Bible that God heals. When we pray with faith, He hears us, and we can be sure He will be merciful. He heals us in many ways, and not always how we expect. If you have cancer or another disease or illness, pray in faith that God will heal you His way, with or without medical intervention.

"He personally carried our sins in his body on the cross so that we can be dead to sin and live for what is right. By his wounds you are healed."
(1 Peter 2:24 NLT)

Prayer

Dear God, we pray for health and wellness over our bodies, minds, and emotions. You created us and told us to ask for your healing when illness strikes. We thank you in advance for your mercy, grace, and healing power. *In Jesus' name, amen.*

Coffee Chat Notes

8

APPRECIATING HUMOR

"Always be humble and gentle. Be patient with
each other, making allowance for each other's faults
because of your love." (Ephesians 4:2 NLT)

I ONCE WORKED AT a funeral home as the lead organist. I had a piano at home, but I wished I had an organ. The beautiful one I had burned in a fire. Practicing the piano at home differed from playing the organ. So, I listed an advertisement in an online buy-and-sell platform's "Looking to Buy" section. I confidently posted, "Looking for a good used organ."

Well—I was not prepared for the quick responses I received in the form of one question or comment after the other—in rapid succession.

"Any particular type of organ?"

"How soon will you need it?"

"Does it need to be in good working order?"

"I may have one in a few years."

"Heart, liver, or kidney?"

"I'll add you to my donor list."

"Good luck, dear."

I was beyond embarrassed, although I learned a valuable lesson. This humbling experience taught me always to be specific in what I ask for, as it will alleviate confusion on the receiving end.

On numerous occasions, we can find humor in poor communication or misunderstandings. Nevertheless, speaking (or typing) clearly is imperative, as we never know whether miscommunication will result in humor or offense.

> "Getting wisdom is the wisest thing you can do! And whatever else you do, develop good judgment." (Proverbs 4:7 NLT)

Prayer

Dear Father in Heaven, thank you for allowing us to see the humor in our everyday lives. We are occasionally amused with the outcome when we fail to communicate accurately. Help us to be more aware of how we convey our inquiries or messages, as we never know how our words will be received. *In Jesus' name, amen.*

COFFEE CHAT NOTES

9

FOCUSING ON THE DESTINATION

> "Look straight ahead and fix your eyes on what lies
> before you. Mark out a straight path for your feet; stay
> on the safe path. Don't get sidetracked; keep your feet
> from following evil."
> (Proverbs 4:25–27 NLT)

LATELY, I HAVE BEEN walking in the evenings to avoid the heat and busy traffic during the day. We live in an area overrun with deer. Most neighbors, including me, would like to see them less frequently. They are cute, yet unfortunately, they eat almost everything we plant and admire. The four-footed furry animals seem to think we are offering them a personal salad bar. We can't blame them, as one of our neighbors routinely feeds them each evening—much to our dismay. After consuming what she offers, the deer wander around looking for other tasty treats.

My backyard burning bush was the last to fall prey to them when autumn was showing off the transformation from dullness to vibrant red.

During one of my walks, I stopped abruptly as two deer dashed out before me. Just as I came to a turn, ready to cross the crosswalk, a huge buck and a doe nearly knocked me over. They were so close I could have touched them. The deer frightened me as they came out between the house and a lawn hedge, making a beeline for the lady's home who feeds them. They were either afraid or starving. Or perhaps the deer thought I would steal their dinner and wanted to get ahead of me. Whatever the case, I was thankful I didn't get run over. I stood there for a few minutes, stunned, envisioning the collision that might have happened but grateful for God's protection. From now on, I must be more alert during my evening walks and be on the lookout for hungry deer.

May we be as laser-focused on pursuing our relationship with God as those deer were on their urgent dinner dash!

"As the deer longs for streams of water, so I long for you, O God."
(Psalm 42:1 NLT)

Prayer

Dear God, help us be so focused on pleasing you that we are not slowed or distracted by what is happening around us. The road we travel leads to the destination You have promised for those who believe in You.
In Jesus' name, amen.

Coffee Chat Notes

10

GETTING BACK UP AFTER FALLING

"...for though the righteous fall seven times, they rise again, but the wicked stumble when calamity strikes."
(Proverbs 24:16)

As a small girl, I loved to run. On summer days, I frequently ran as fast as possible on the gravel road in front of our house. My mother repeatedly admonished me to stop running because I would fall. Sure enough, I frequently hit the unforgiving roadway while still in motion. As a result, I was often a wounded little sprinter, having skinned my knees, elbows, and hands.

I knew my mother was watching from the kitchen window, so I lay on the stony, dusty ground, crying, waiting for her to help me. I could hear her yelling in the distance, "Get back up!" I would slowly hobble up or wait until she came to my aid. Soon, I would be back outside, patched up and ready for new adventures. The bruises and scrapes on my knees seemed more severe because we little girls always wore dresses back then, even outside to play. I sported those bandages with pride and pomp as if they were beauty pageant awards. Once out on the stony-laden road again, I would be off running, with the breeze loosening the ribbon in my hair and causing the lacey collar on my dress to flap against my face.

With alarming regularity, we adults stumble as we tread through our days. Life can be challenging, and we often face setbacks that cause us to lose our footing. We usually get back up on our own when we tumble. Other times, we cannot because our injuries are too extensive, so we whimper over our wounds. Sometimes, an emotional or unseen wound, such as a broken heart, knocks us down. Occasionally, we wait in our misery for help to arrive. However, we can't stay down; we must rise and get back into the game of life. Still, sometimes, groveling in the dirt is easier.

We will run again, even if we are all bandaged up from the last time we hit rock bottom. Like an attentive parent watching over us, God gives us the strength to get back after a fall—lovingly and gently heals our wounds and, in many cases, sends another to our aid.

Life may have dealt us a tremendous blow that knocked us off course, causing harm to our hearts and souls. God will come to our rescue in due time. He sees us and is keenly aware of our pain, suffering, and predicament.

The next time we fall, finding ourselves bruised and broken, let's ask our Heavenly Father for help. In addition to helping us get back up, He will apply His unlimited supply of God-sized bandages as needed! We can then resume our journey under His ever-watchful eye.

> "He heals the broken hearted and bandages their wounds."
> (Psalm 147:3 NLT)

Prayer

Dear Heavenly Father, help us recover and continue life's race after a fall. You will give us another chance and a fresh new start. Thank you for always being with us, helping us get back up when we fall, and mending our heartaches and injuries. *In Jesus' name, amen.*

COFFEE CHAT NOTES

11

DARING TO DREAM

> "Hope deferred makes the heart sick, but a dream fulfilled is a tree of life." (Proverbs 13:12 NLT)

During or after significant life challenges such as addiction, a cancer diagnosis, or divorce, we question our purpose. Too often, thoughts of dreaming about what we planned and hoped life would look like are brushed aside to make room for more pressing matters.

What have we always wanted to do but didn't? What is near and dear to our hearts? Did we dream of playing the piano, guitar, or violin? Do we have a story safely tucked in our souls, waiting to be shared? Have we ever longed to create, perhaps to paint beautiful landscapes, or sew our own fashion designs? Maybe we once desired to develop our inner chef, write a book, take gorgeous photographs, sing to our heart's content, or learn about make-up artistry.

Now could be the perfect time to dig deep into our hearts and entertain those dreams again. Do we dare?

Just because we are *broken* in some fashion does not mean our God-given purpose is squashed. We are still *beloved*! Our brokenness is a part of our journey. It does not define us. We must ask ourselves what has always been in our hearts, perhaps placed there by God, even though hidden for a while.

Dare to dream again; we should. Dare to dream again; we must!

> "Take delight in the Lord, and he will give you the desires of your heart." (Psalms 37:4)

Prayer

Dear Lord, You are the giver of dreams. You frequently inspire us with dreams of what You have planned for us. Help us to pursue the dreams that align with Your Word. *In Jesus' name, amen.*

COFFEE CHAT NOTES

12

COPING WITH UNFAIRNESS

> "So don't be afraid; you are more valuable to God
> than a whole flock of sparrows."
> (Matthew 10:31 NLT)

HAVE YOU EVER FELT the sting of unfairness? Do you sometimes feel at a disadvantage? Having that frame of mind is common when in a place of brokenness. Recently, while sitting at a picnic table outside a fast-food restaurant, I noticed a most unfair situation unfolding.

A flock of sparrows was actively scurrying for lunch on the grass. A little birdie caught my eye. It was hopping instead of running like the others. Upon looking closer, I noticed that this bird was disadvantaged by having just one leg. Each time the flock spotted food, they ran, flew, and did whatever they could to get there before the others, including the hopping bird. One would think that the able-bodied birds would accommodate a slower one because of a visible disadvantage. However, they did not save even a food remnant for that poor little bird. It was every man for himself—or, I should say—every sparrow.

As I thought about the challenging life for the one-legged sparrow, I remembered the Bible tells us that God takes care of the sparrows as He cares for us. So, how should we cope when facing unfairness? Even though it seems we are left behind or shut out because of a disadvantage, our Heavenly Father sees us and cares. I noted that while visible or invisible limitations can challenge us, He often shows His care for us through others. If not, He looks after us in ways beyond what we can hope for, as He did for this little sparrow. God promises a double portion of inheritance for those who have experienced shame and disgrace due to unfair treatment. And even when we feel alone or abandoned, our faith sustains us, giving us the fortitude to carry on. You may be disadvantaged unfairly, but you are not disqualified from all God has planned for you.

"Instead of your shame you will receive a double portion, and instead of disgrace you will rejoice in your inheritance. And so you will inherit a double portion in your land, and everlasting joy will be yours."
(Isaiah 61:7)

PRAYER

Dear God, You never promised us this earthly life would be fair. You see the overall picture, and we do not. Help us trust that the unfair situations we often find ourselves in are only a part of the whole plan and purpose You have for us. *In Jesus' name, amen.*

COFFEE CHAT NOTES

13

ENJOYING LIFE

"This is the day the Lord has made; We will rejoice and be glad in it." (Psalm 118:24 NKJV)

HAVE YOU EVER WITNESSED a scene that made your day? My husband and I were walking on a nearby path specifically for walkers and cyclists. We heard pleasant-sounding music before we saw her. Coming toward us was a mature woman with a helmet, gloves, streamers, and a smile as big as all outdoors! She was riding her bicycle with a ghetto blaster in the front parcel carrier, blaring with her music of choice. Josh Groban and Celine Dion singing "The Prayer" was music to our ears! She waved as she came closer to us, going in the opposite direction. After a smile from us, she continued on her way. We chuckled then and still do when we remember the incident. Here was a woman living *her best life*, doing what made her happy.

Do we intentionally include activities that bring joy and happiness into our daily routine? If not, we should. This woman inspired us as she displayed her cheer. We may not choose to ride a bicycle with our music blasting for all to hear, but something must bring us great joy. We should ponder that thought for a moment to discover if we are missing out on anything that would bring that kind of smile to our faces.

> "A cheerful heart is good medicine, but a crushed spirit dries up the bones." (Proverbs 17:22)

Prayer

Dear God, You desire that we enjoy life as You tell us in Your Word, the Bible. Help us seek ways to relax and appreciate the world when possible. Even though many things are happening in the world that bring sadness to our hearts, may we rejoice in Your goodness, enjoying the opportunities afforded us. *In Jesus' name, amen.*

COFFEE CHAT NOTES

14

STAYING ROOTED AND GROUNDED

> "Remain in me as I also remain in you. No branch
> can bear fruit by itself; it must remain in the vine.
> Neither can you bear fruit unless you remain in me.
> I am the vine; you are the branches. If you remain in
> me and I in you, you will bear much fruit; apart from
> me, you can do nothing. If you do not remain in me,
> you are like a branch that is thrown away and withers;
> such branches are picked up, thrown into the fire, and
> burned. If you remain in me and my words remain in
> you, ask whatever you wish, and it will be done for
> you. This is to my Father's glory that you bear much
> fruit, showing yourselves to be my disciples."
> (John 15:4–8)

AS I INSPECTED THE leafy bush in my yard, I pondered whether it was a lilac bush. *After all, there were no lilacs on it! Isn't a lilac bush supposed to have lilacs? Eventually,* I thought. *Yet, it sure is taking a long time!* I loved the fragrance of lilacs and was becoming impatient after several seasons of waiting for that splash of purple in my flower bed. I was disappointed with the bush's inability to produce the desired flower. I felt it was in a good location, with just enough light and water. So, what was the problem? I began to look deeper! Much deeper! I had the answer, or so I thought. Maybe it was dreaded root rot! If the roots aren't healthy, the bush will not be healthy. Perhaps I should relocate the plant to an area with richer soil, more water, and sunlight and fertilize it. Maybe I could prune the branches that look less likely to flower. *I had to do something to get this bush to produce what it was meant to produce.*

Having done all the above, I left my lilac bush alone. I did all I could. However, I got some fake lilacs and stuck them in among the bushy leaves. It looked like the real deal, especially from a distance, but it did not have the fragrance familiar to genuine lilacs.

I got to thinking that if a bush has a faulty root system, it would be lifeless, dehydrated, dry/parched, fruitless/flowerless, unsightly, weak, starving/dying, in need of pruning, blown about with every storm, unneeded/unwanted and finally uprooted. *This was not the case with my bush, as it looked healthy, green, and lush.*

On the contrary, if a bush were well nourished by its roots, it would be upright/strong, able to withstand the winds/storms without wavering, vibrant/attractive, green/lush/healthy-looking, bearing fruit/flowers, growing towards the light, able to draw nourishment from the roots, and beautiful. *This described my bush!*

I was perplexed! *So, where were the lilacs?* All that was lacking were the actual flowers that would prove to me that it was, in fact, a lilac bush.

After all this wondering and reasoning, I decided to check on the bush. You guessed it! The wind had blown the fake lilacs away! Upon looking closer, I saw numerous lilac buds just waiting to bloom to show off their beautiful purple attire and share their sweet fragrance. Beholding the beauty of my lilac bush led me to my original question of whether a bush is a lilac bush because it has lilacs or if it has lilacs because it's a lilac bush. That day, I learned an important lesson—*it has lilacs because it's a lilac bush.* It is indeed the root system that determines the type of bush. In this case, the lilacs were the visible evidence and proof.

We can all draw valuable conclusions and life lessons from all of this. Things are only sometimes as they appear or appear not to be.

- Fakeness will always be blown away.

- Anything valuable is worth waiting for.

- The root system determines the fruit of a plant.

- Beauty and purpose come from being rooted and grounded correctly.

- Just because the fruit or flower does not appear quickly doesn't mean the roots are not preparing to present the fruit or flower in its own time.

We are admonished and encouraged to be rooted in the Bible, our spiritual nourishment, and to be fruitful in doing good works according to His will. We don't have to strive, work, or worry about bearing spiritual fruit. It will be an automatic result of abiding in His Word. Remember that the lilac bush doesn't stress out, strain, or work to produce the lilacs. Instead, it waits until the time is right, trusting that the lilacs will appear in due season if it stays well connected to the roots.

"But blessed is the one who trusts in the Lord, whose confidence is in him. They will be like a tree planted by the water that sends out its roots by the stream. It does not fear when heat comes; its leaves are always green. It has no worries in a year of drought and never fails to bear fruit." (Jeremiah 17:7–8)

Prayer

Dear Heavenly Father, we ask that You help us stay rooted and grounded in Your Word. It is the lifeline for anything of value we do for You. Communion with You in prayer helps our root system to thrive, thereby becoming who You created us to be. *In Jesus' name, amen.*

COFFEE CHAT NOTES

15

LAMENTING THE PAST

"You will keep in perfect peace all who trust in you, all whose thoughts are fixed on you." (Isaiah 26:3 NLT)

UNDERSTANDABLY, WE MAY BE saddled with unpleasant emotions at any time on our journey. Memories of past traumas can threaten to flood our minds, and, feeling unsettled, we may overreact. Instead, let's allow these laments to provide more traction to keep going.

We, who have just come through devastating losses, know that a listening ear is all we need most days. Someone to sit with us in our grief is comforting. Talking about our feelings soothes our souls and temporarily lifts our load. Since the experience of grief is not linear, fluctuating feelings of loss can often surprise us. We can experience loss and trauma in both extreme and subtle ways. From moving to a new location, a job change, illness, losing a long-time friendship, or, at the very worst, suffering from the death of a loved one—our perception of life can be gravely altered. There are many additional events that can trigger ongoing feelings of loss, both one-time and ongoing.

Now and again, we carry grievances with us for comfort as if to protect them. We nurse feelings of loss, clinging to our laments as a child hugs a ratty old blanket. The child prefers the familiarity of the ragged one when a parent tries to replace it with a fresh one. Denying we are clinging to trying to understand our past will not serve us well. Reading God's Word and praying for direction brings hope to our hearts, even as memories of loss cause us to sing the blues now and then. We may agree that *memories could be the sweetest thing on this side of Heaven or the worst on this side of hell.* We need God's help managing our memories—not letting them randomly consume our thoughts. As we continue our journey, we will hopefully loosen our grip on those hard memories and release them into God's caring hands.

Some of our laments may be:

- Life is not fair.

- How did I get here?

- I tried; I really did.

- Why did this happen?

- Why my loved one?

- It was so sudden.

- I didn't have the opportunity to say goodbye.

- What now?

- I thought I was making the right choice.

- Why did I have to suffer so much?

- No one cares or understands my pain.

- The house is so empty without him.

- I don't deserve this.

- Does God see me; does He even care?

- I have no one to talk to. I am so lonely.

- Maybe this is all I deserve.

"And now, dear brother and sisters, one final thing. Fix your thoughts on what is true, and honorable, and right, and pure, and lovely, and admirable; think about things that are excellent and worthy of praise." (Philippians 4:8 NLT)

Prayer

Dear Lord, You are the only One who can heal our *broken* hearts after we experience traumas, losses, and grief. As we lament and grieve past hurts, help us come to You for comfort. Even though we don't understand why we had to face the overwhelming pain, we know You care and will always and forever be there for us. *In Jesus' name, amen.*

COFFEE CHAT NOTES

16

WANTING TO QUIT AND GO BACK

"Brothers and sisters, I do not consider myself yet to have taken hold of it. But one thing I do; Forgetting what is behind and straining toward what is ahead, I press on toward the goal to win the prize for which God has called me heavenward in Christ Jesus." (Philippians 3:13–14)

COURAGEOUSNESS IS NOT NECESSARILY finishing the project or quieting the storm. It does not only consist of being victorious in your attempts to overcome or win. When the core of your being shouts: *Just quit already. Why continue to humiliate yourself? The way forward is too difficult. The mountain is too high, and the valley is too deep. What were you thinking? You are not up to the task, so why try to tough it out? Just admit failure and settle.*

You may have experienced those agonizing thought patterns; I know I have. Bravery is lifting your head again and facing the confusion, chaos, and fear head-on. It is refusing to give up while navigating seemingly insurmountable obstacles. You may have to regroup, take a short detour, or make a rest stop, but do not give up! Determination and grit to keep going require laying down the props, forsaking comfort, abandoning the desire for predictable outcomes, and staring down what seems impossible to take out or overcome.

Let's do the next right thing, no matter how insignificant it may seem. God rewards our faith, trust, and obedience. We have come too far and have been through too much to quit. There is a story in Exodus 14:5–28 about God's people, the Israelites, who were at the edge of the Red Sea and wanted to return to Egypt. With God's direction, Moses pleaded with Pharoah to let the people go after they had been in slavery in Egypt for four hundred years. Once free, they wanted to return to captivity rather than drown in the sea stretching before them. Little did they know God was about to part the sea so they could cross on dry ground.

Obstacles can block our way at every turn, and we often encounter Red Seas of our own. Yet, venturing toward the unknown is usually better than quitting or returning to the familiar.

> "Let us not become weary in doing good, for at the proper time, we will reap a harvest if we do not give up." (Galatians 6:9)

Prayer

Dear God, so many times, we want to quit when the road of life seems too strenuous to manage. Even though the path behind us may have been troublesome, at least it was familiar. Facing the unknown is often frightful as we do not know what to expect. This is when we come to You, Father God, asking for grace and mercy for the past and confidence and faith for the future. *In Jesus' name, amen.*

COFFEE CHAT NOTES

17

PURSUING PEACE

> "May the God of hope fill you with all joy and
> peace as you trust in him so that you may overflow
> with hope by the power of the Holy Spirit."
> (Romans 15:13)

HOW CAN WE HAVE peace or joy in this ever-changing world fraught with confusion and wariness? There's a story in Mark 4:35–39 of Jesus in a boat with His disciples as a ferocious storm whipped up the waves. With water in the boat, they found Jesus asleep. Waking Him, they cried, "Teacher, don't you care that we are going to drown?" When Jesus woke up, He rebuked the wind and said to the waves, "Silence, be still!"

Like those disciples, I wondered where Jesus was in my *personal* storm. When I prayed to Him to calm the threatening waves, I felt He was right there with me. The waves did not immediately subside, yet I was reassured that God was the One who would ultimately bring peace to my restless heart, calming the storm in His time.

When we are in a storm of fear and uncertainty, our sole reassurance comes from knowing that God is the only One who can bring peace to our troubled hearts. God says He will give us peace that the world can't provide. He admonishes us not to be afraid. As we look to the future, bracing for what comes next, let's put our faith and reliance on God and His Word, the Bible. He is the sovereign One who can get us through trepidation with a peace He alone can give.

"Peace, I leave with you; my peace I give you. I do not give to you as the world gives. Do not let your hearts be troubled and do not be afraid."
(John 14:27)

Prayer

Dear Lord, You alone can give us peace beyond what we understand or imagine. In the trying times of uncertainty and fear of what may happen next in this world of sin and darkness, help us pray for Your peace. You will give us perfect peace when we pursue You, the Giver of peace. *In Jesus' name, amen.*

COFFEE CHAT NOTES

18

TRUSTING GOD'S PROMISES

> "Trust in the Lord with all your heart and lean not on
> your own understanding; in all your ways, submit to
> him, and he will make your paths straight."
> (Proverbs 3:5–6)

REMEMBER VISITS TO GRANDMA'S house and being told to look but don't touch as you walked past her rose garden? *Weren't rose gardens just for grandmas?* I thought so as a child. There was a clear rationale for why we were discouraged from getting too close to the rosebushes. Those bushes have prickly surprises awaiting unsuspecting admirers. However, the blossoms were colorful and fragrant, adding warmth and a welcoming touch to grandma's green space.

It is inconceivable to have lush roses without pesky thorns, light without darkness, joy without pain, mountaintop experiences without valleys, or sunshine without rain. While we marvel at the *impossibilities,* we trust God has created our world with perfect precision.

A woman who appeared to have more thorns than roses in her life: Beautiful enough to be a movie star, she lived a relatively obscure life in a small town. Having married young, she had two equally attractive daughters. Before the girls were grown, her husband passed, leaving her to raise them independently. Her daughters were not yet old enough to marry or have children when they were taken from her in a tragic accident. She would later remarry, only to become a widow once more. Shortly after losing her second husband, she reflected on the blessings evident in her life and how she had plenty to be thankful for. She can be seen walking (alone) in her neighborhood these days. A genuine and heartfelt smile is graciously given to anyone she meets. She was not handed a rose garden in life, but despite it all, she was grateful for the solitary roses she could admire or attain along the way. She kept them close to her heart while they were hers to hold.

What unique and precious *roses* have we held on to as we trusted God's promises, provision, and plan? Did we miss them while looking for the entire garden? Let's appreciate the blessings on our journey, as we never know how long they will be ours to treasure. God promises to be with us, whether in an entire rose garden, holding a single rose, or left empty-handed. He will never leave or forsake us if we rely on Him to comfort us. We can securely lean and rely on His promises.

> "When I am afraid, I put my trust in you." (Psalm 56:3)

Prayer

Dear Lord, we know Your Word tells us to trust You. We want to, yet sometimes we bemoan our circumstances. Let us determine in our hearts to trust You, even when life gives us the *proverbial lemons. In Jesus' name, amen.*

COFFEE CHAT NOTES

19

PUTTING THE PIECES BACK TOGETHER

> "And the God of all grace, who called you to his
> eternal glory in Christ, after you have suffered a
> little while, will himself restore you and make you
> strong, firm, and steadfast." (1 Peter 5:10)

AT AGE FOURTEEN, I started making a quilt. My Sunday school teacher wanted to give us, her class of young teenage girls, something to do on a Friday night, so she started a quilting class. I did not want to go, yet I went to see my Sunday school friends.

Mrs. L., our teacher, asked us to gather all the unused material from our mothers' sewing projects, as we would be making a *crazy quilt*. Since we were learning how to sew in a home economics class at junior high school, we also had stray pieces from whatever we made. So, we took our little scrap bags of material and some different colors of sewing floss with us on that first Friday night.

The random pieces of fabric with all colors, shapes, and designs were assembled with basting thread without a pattern. The ragged and uneven edges where each piece met another were decorated with sewing floss stitched in a matching color before the backing was attached. *That's why it is called a crazy quilt.* We looked forward to our weekly quilting classes throughout every one of the three months. Mrs. L. always made it fun with treats and stories from her youth. Then, when it was time for the quilting group to disband, we were proud of our creations, even though none of us would likely finish them. We may have established and attended the world's youngest quilting bee.

I still have that unfinished quilt, which reminds me of my incomplete life of stray, jagged, and uneven pieces still being put together. The quilt pieces were once a part of another piece of work. When put together, it is a reconstruction of detached remnants of a past garment, presented as a beautiful *piece of work!* I had a co-worker at the bank who vividly described one of our customers. After waiting on him, she would say, "Now there goes a *piece of work.*" It was not a compliment; we gathered.

When we surrender our shattered lives to God in prayer, we become a work in progress as He reattaches our *broken* pieces, grafting and stitching us into the person He created us to be. When we are God's *piece of work*, it is a compliment!

"And we know that in all things, God works for the good of those who love him, who have been called according to his purpose."
(Romans 8:28)

Prayer

Dear God, sometimes we are so *broken* that we feel like we are in pieces! Help us offer and surrender our brokenness to You prayerfully. Since You have created us, You know how to restore and mend us. Thank you. *In Jesus' name, amen.*

COFFEE CHAT NOTES

20

LIGHTING THE WAY

"Your Word is a lamp to guide my feet and a light for my path." (Psalm 119:105 NLT)

AS A SKINCARE AND makeup consultant, I attended the grandest company event of the year in Toronto, Canada. In the closing session, with thousands in attendance, each woman was given a small unlit candle. With dimmed lights, the woman with the first lit candle shared the flame with the next, lighting one candle at a time. It was a soul-stirring moment as the coliseum gradually lightened—with thousands of candles shining brightly. It all began with the light from one solitary candle. This event was reminiscent of how the world shares light and love, one person at a time, on many occasions.

The gospel message is compared to light numerous times in the Bible. The "Light" of the Gospel shines, diminishing the darkness. The contrast between dark and light helps us see the next step on our path.

Since the next step is our only one, it makes sense to shine a light on it, even with a flashlight or a candle. Before we receive light, our circumstances are routinely darkest. Then, just as dawn breaks and the fog clears, we behold the light that was always there. So, the sun perpetually shines, even when shrouded by clouds, fog, or the darkness of night for intermittent periods.

Keeping our eyes on our path is more straightforward with sufficient light, preferably from the sun, as that light is all-encompassing, helping us see all around us. However, if we are lighting our way with a flashlight, we must not shine the beam of light too far ahead. Doing so may cause us to overlook the next step, tripping over the stone under our foot and taking an unnecessary tumble. We require just enough light for the next step while glancing ahead periodically to see the bigger picture of where we are going.

God's Word is our "Light" in darkness, showing us the way. So, we must soldier on while it is still day with faith that the "Light" will brighten our pathway, even when we do not visibly see it or feel its warmth. Rest assured, there will be enough light to keep going, one day at a time, one step at a time, and one moment at a time. Then, with an eye on the proverbial light at the end of the tunnel, we will find our way forward. Sometimes, we may even have light shared with us from a candle.

> "The light shines in the darkness, and the darkness can never extinguish it." (John 1:5 NLT)

Prayer

Dear God, we know You are the "Light" of the world. Please help us allow your presence to lighten our path. Illuminate our journey as we read Your Word. Give us the desire to let the light You have given us shine in this dark world. *In Jesus' name, amen.*

COFFEE CHAT NOTES

21

HIDING NO MORE

> "The Lord is my light and my salvation; whom shall I fear? The Lord is the stronghold of my life; of whom shall I be afraid?" (Psalm 27:1)

LONG BEFORE WE STARTED school, we may have been familiar with the game of hide-and-seek. Later, we may have played the game with our children or those we cared for. As adults, however, hiding is less fun. We may hide in our brokenness—not under the bed, behind the sofa, or from actual or perceived danger—but in plain sight. Instead of hiding behind a chair or in the next room, waiting excitedly to be found, we often languish for years, hiding from the truth or our present reality. We hide from the fear of being found out. *We hide because of unfounded fear.*

Our stay in the metaphorical cocoon is often more extended than necessary because of insecurity or a desire to be more acceptable or prepared to enter our next life stage. Only when we take that leap of faith will we be able to live the life we were created to live. God never created us, His daughters, to hide in our hard places. We often hide in obscurity because we feel we don't measure up to what others thought we should be or would be.

The devil tries to divide and separate us from others. Not only does he try to steal our God-given calling, desires, and dreams, but also our connection with others. He wants us to live alone and in fear of judgment. He wants us to sit in solitude with toxic thoughts tormenting us instead of in a relationship with others who can help soothe our aching hearts.

God has given us His Word, promises, and the Holy Spirit so we can stand firm and reclaim what we have lost in all our hiding. God's Word is a sword against the enemy's tactics against us. The more we hide His Word in our hearts, the more we can stand against the enemy. God longs to restore us to His comfort and safety. He is our soft place to fall. We can hold our heads high and our shoulders back because God loves us, always has, and always will. He accepts us as we are, helping us avoid harmful and unnecessary hiding.

While it is always possible to stop hiding and start living, it will undoubtedly require stepping out of our comfort zone. Yet it will be worth it, as we were created for healthy, meaningful interaction with others.

"But those who do what is right come to the light so others can see that they are doing what God wants." (John 3:21 NLT)

Prayer

Dear Heavenly Father, You do not intend us to hide from others. Help us acknowledge that we are masterpieces in Your sight and learn how to live as the beautiful women You have created. *In Jesus' name, amen.*

COFFEE CHAT NOTES

22

RE-EVALUATING REJECTION

> "He was in the world, and though the world was made through him, the world did not recognize him. He came to that which was his own, but his own did not receive him." (John 1:10–11)

A DONKEY'S OWNER WANTED to put him down because he was old and not of much value anymore. However, since the owner didn't have the heart to shoot the donkey, he asked a neighbor to throw him into a hole in the ground that had been used for garbage disposal. The neighbor agreed. Later, as people threw refuse into the pit, it fell on top of the donkey, who would shake it off and step up onto the growing mound. The donkey kept stepping up as the garbage piled up until he was ground level. Then he walked away. Taking a lesson from this donkey, instead of wallowing in the trash that sometimes gets dumped on us in the way of rejection, we can shake it off, step up, walk away, and stay the course. *Of course, this is easier said than done.*

It always hurts to be overlooked for positions or desired jobs that we are qualified for and left out of places or groups where we think we belong. And when we are shunned and overlooked at our place of employment, church, circle of friends, or even family, we feel disheartened. When we are knocked down and shut out more often than we can count, trying so hard to be one of the crowd, we often feel we don't measure up. We may have even ventured on a journey of learning to love ourselves and others, only to have been overlooked and rejected. When I faced rejection, I was often advised to develop a *thick skin*. On the contrary, I typically retreated, cowering in self-pity.

However, even though we feel terrible when left out and rejected, it can allow us to try to understand the cause or meaning. We may even discover that those rejecting us were as *broken* as we were, and their rejection of us had more to do with their insecurities. Once we gain valuable discernment, although difficult, we can choose to strengthen our resilience from this point forward.

When looking at the life of Jesus, we read that He, too, was ostracized and rejected. The verse quoted below says He was *despised*—such a strong word. So, when we feel the sting of rejection, we know God understands our pain.

> "He was despised and rejected by mankind, a man of suffering and familiar with pain. Like one from whom people hide their faces, he was despised, and we held him in low esteem." (Isaiah 53:3)

PRAYER

Dear God in Heaven, we come to You for comfort when rejected. You have experienced rejection far more significant than anything we could ever imagine. Thank you for enduring the suffering and shame of the cross for our salvation. We love You. *In Jesus' name, amen.*

COFFEE CHAT NOTES

23

FOLLOWING THE SHEPHERD

"The Lord is my Shepherd; I lack nothing. He makes me lie down in green pastures; he leads me beside quiet waters; he refreshes my soul. He guides me along the right paths for his name's sake. Even though I walk through the darkest valley, I will fear no evil, for you are with me; your rod and your staff they comfort me. You prepare a table before me in the presence of my enemies. You anoint my head with oil, my cup overflows. Surely your goodness and love will follow me all the days of my life, and I will dwell in the house of the Lord forever." (Psalm 23)

THIS PSALM IS OFTEN quoted at funerals because it is so comforting. It is a Psalm of David, a shepherd boy who later becomes a king. In these verses, the Bible refers to us as sheep and Jesus as "The Good Shepherd." In our *broken* places, as we journey to wholeness, the idea of us being the sheep and Jesus as our "Shepherd" is soothing to our souls.

I learned much from a woman who was the wife of a sheep rancher. In this Psalm, we read that Jesus anoints our heads with oil. I never understood what that meant until the sheep rancher's wife explained the concept of anointing a sheep's head with oil. Having extensive knowledge of the ways of sheep, she told me that sheep keepers, especially those in warmer climates, will often put protective oil on the sheep's head to protect them from nose flies. If the flies get up the nostrils of a sheep, it can cause them to go mad. The idea of our "Shepherd" anointing our heads with oil symbolizes how He protects us from the enemy's attacks and lies.

Sheep need a shepherd to protect and guide them because they are timid, defenseless, and blind followers. In addition, their strong will and independent nature can threaten their safety.

I have written several characteristics of sheep and shepherds. The list is incomplete, as you may think of others. Notice how the characteristics and relationship between the sheep and shepherd are reminiscent of us and our Shepherd, Jesus.

Characteristics of sheep:

- One fearful sheep makes them all afraid.

- If they get their heads stuck in a fence, they can't get out.

- If woolly sheep land on their backs, they can't get up.

- If caught in a thicket on the edge of a hill or cliff, they are doomed without help and may meet their demise if they go over the edge.

- They will overgraze an area.
- They will get lost and often follow other lost sheep.
- They will not survive without a shepherd.
- The shepherd's voice is familiar and comforting to them.
- They won't lie down if they are afraid.
- They need quiet streams to drink from so they can hear possible danger.

Characteristics of the shepherd:

- Guides the sheep to safe and green pastures.
- Provides food and leads them to quiet streams of water.
- Anoints the heads of the sheep with oil.
- Knows when one in the flock is missing.
- Looks for and rescues the one who is lost.
- Is the gatekeeper who protects the sheep from danger.
- Corrects them with a rod and staff.
- Corrals them at night.

> "All of us, like sheep, have strayed away. We have left God's path to follow our own." (Isaiah 53:6 NLT)

PRAYER

Dear Heavenly Father, we have all gone astray and followed our own path. Please help us repent and follow You as sheep follow their shepherd. To follow You, we need to read the Bible and pray to commune with You. We praise and thank You for being our good "Shepherd." You guide, protect, comfort, and rescue us when we fall into temptation or get lost on the side of an embankment somewhere. *In Jesus' name, amen.*

COFFEE CHAT NOTES

24

DISCERNING HEART MATTERS

"Guard your heart above all else, for it determines the
course of your life." (Proverbs 4:23 NLT)

HAVE YOU EVER MET someone who seemed heartless? You may remember "The Wizard of Oz," a popular and timeless movie in which there was a character without a heart called the "Tin Man." He desperately wanted a heart to know happiness and the human experience.

Since we all have hearts, taking heart inventory will assure us of being in a healthy emotional place. As a bank teller, I observed something compelling about older folks. Some allowed life to make them sweet and gracious. Others grew older with a sense of entitlement, exhibiting a mean side of their personality. Some were bitter, unforgiving, and angry—impatient and demanding.

I learned we must uproot bitterness early so it doesn't grow into irreparable flaws as we mature, guarding our hearts at all costs. Our hearts are where love, wisdom, and kindness should live.

From birth, we constantly make downloads into our hearts and uploads from our hearts. Since what we allow to reside there will eventually come out, we must do a regular heart check. Then, with a complete overhaul or house (heart) cleaning, we can deal with accumulated poor attitudes, bitterness, or skewed ways of thinking. We make headway toward our dreams, goals, and purpose when fully embracing, uploading, offloading, or deleting damaging programs.

"Search me, God, and know my heart; test me and know my anxious thoughts. Point out anything in me that offends you and lead me along the path of everlasting life." (Psalm 139:23–24 NLT)

Prayer

Dear God, our hearts are at the center of our being. Without You, the Bible tells us our hearts are deceitfully wicked (Jeremiah 17:9). Help us guard our hearts from wickedness by allowing Your Holy Spirit to convict and cleanse us of anything harmful to our walk with You. May we be careful to lay down any destructive words, thoughts, or behaviors that are not pleasing to You. *In Jesus' name, amen.*

COFFEE CHAT NOTES

25

FACING DISAPPOINTMENTS

> "And this hope will not lead to disappointment. For we know how dearly God loves us, because he has given us the Holy Spirit to fill our hearts with his love." (Romans 5:5 NLT)

"How would you like to go on a cruise?" My friend asked as we pulled out of her driveway and headed to a local thrift store. "Me, go on a cruise?" How could she have known that such a dream had been on my bucket list? Plans were finalized in the following weeks for a dream-come-true excursion. As the departure date drew near, we were saddened when the tour company canceled the trip. Disheartening!

What cancelations or disappointments have you faced? We can be disappointed in ourselves, others, and God. We are not alone when we feel this way, as these emotions are common. Occasionally, when things go in a different direction than we thought or hoped, it can be a blessing in hindsight.

Life's disappointments are harsh and laborious to bear at times, but we do not have to succumb to their weight. When we face them head-on, not brushing them aside, we can better handle them and move forward in peace. Asking for God's comfort and direction in these times alleviates our dismay and helps us adjust and heal.

> "The Lord is close to the brokenhearted and saves those who are crushed in spirit." (Psalm 34:18)

Prayer

Dear God, it is impossible to live without facing disappointments. Help us deal with challenges as You would want. Help us realize this world is not perfect, and we can expect disappointments to come our way. Thank you for walking beside us in these potentially upsetting situations. *In Jesus' name, amen.*

COFFEE CHAT NOTES

26

FLOURISHING IN THE VALLEYS

"Even when I walk through the darkest valley, I will not be afraid, for You are close beside me. Your rod and your staff protect and comfort me."
(Psalm 23:4 NLT)

WE ALL TRAVEL THROUGH valleys in this journey called life. When we face an illness, a relationship fracture, a financial crisis, or any other low place, it is confirmation that life is not lived solely on the mountaintops. To have mountaintops, we need valleys.

We venture into many high and low experiences. The high or mountaintop happenings could include a new job, a wedding, the birth of a baby, a graduation, a retirement, a clean bill of health after a medical ordeal, and many other events. The lows and valley experiences could include a prolonged illness, a breach in a relationship, the loss of a job, or worse, the loss of a loved one. Many other harsh realities could be included here.

We have heard that growth happens in the valleys. The valleys are well-watered after the rain descends from the mountains, making them lush with greenery. Can our valley circumstances result in a time of growth? We would love to flourish on the mountaintops, happily skipping from one to the other without ever sliding into the valleys. However, God knew it would not be the healthiest way to live. We need the valley experiences to appreciate the mountaintop highs and to prevent us from developing a sense of pride. Self-sufficiency could also occur if we lived only on the high summits of life.

> "For I know the thoughts that I think towards you, says the Lord, thoughts of peace and not of evil, to give you a future and a hope."
> (Jeremiah 29:11 NKJV)

Prayer

Dear God, help us glean all the lessons we can in the valleys. We flourish when we depend on You for our way through them. You promised to protect and comfort us when we encounter the valleys of life. We thank You, Lord. *In Jesus' name, amen.*

COFFEE CHAT NOTES

27

BELIEVING IN MIRACLES

"For he will command his angels concerning you
to guard you in all your ways." (Psalm 91:11)

OUR COMPACT, CREAM-COLORED VEHICLE huffed and puffed on the dirt road. My parents, brother, and I were on an adventure—a day trip to the countryside. The ground beneath us was slick and slippery from earlier heavy rain. In the backseat, my little brother entertained himself with his toy cars. I was also in the back but chose to stand on the hump in the middle of the floor. (This was long before the mandatory seatbelt law.) I wanted a clear view of the road ahead, which was becoming dangerous. My parents tried to stay calm but were uneasy and tense. Trying to make it through deep ruts and muck, Dad gripped the steering wheel tightly, pressing his foot on the gas pedal to gain traction and momentum.

Without warning, a sickening, bumpy thud stopped the car, sending me tumbling to the floor! Muddy water splashed on the car windows. We were quiet and still while Dad got out to assess the situation. He discovered that the incident was not a minor mishap. Our itty-bitty car was solidly mired in the ditch and tipped to one side. Unable to open the passenger-side doors, we climbed up the grey vinyl seats and slid into Dad's arms. Once outside the car, our shoes absorbed gobs of guck as we sank into the sludge! What a mess! The tires on the passenger side were firmly wedged, hugged snuggly by massive mounds of thick, heavy mud.

A man of deep faith, Dad clicked his tongue with concern. Praying to God for help, he gazed towards the heavens, shook his head, rubbed his chin, and cried aloud, "Dear God, how are we going to get out of this ditch?" Near our unintentional parking spot, houses were few and far between. Fields, rocks, and trees silently witnessed our predicament, unable to help. Chirping birds were oblivious to our distress. We stood by while Dad took another look at our dire straits. Yup—our ride was stuck in the middle of nowhere! *Suddenly, we heard a thunderous rumble and felt the ground shake.*

Looking away from our muddy mishap, we saw the biggest truck I had ever seen. The giant wheels towered beside me when it came to a stop near us. A man opened the large door and jumped down from the step on the side of the truck. "I see you need help!" Without another word, he grabbed a hefty length of rope and attached one end to the bumper of the monster truck and the other to the fender of our now-dwarfed car. He climbed back into his gigantic rig, and with one jolt, we were back up on the road. Wow! We observed, with shock, the deep ruts where the tires had been moments earlier. Suddenly, Dad swung his hands, "Where did he go? How could he have left that fast? I didn't even get a chance to thank him!"

The truck vanished into thin air without a rumble, and there was no sight of it on the road in either direction—it simply disappeared without a trace. I firmly believe God sent an angel to our little family that day. An angel who could drive a big *ole* rumbling truck!

Think of a time when God may have sent an angel to protect you or your family. Revel in the majesty of that miracle for a few moments today and remember God's goodness, especially when situations are grim or just plain terrible.

> "Are not all angels ministering spirits sent to serve those who will inherit salvation?" (Hebrews 1:14)

Prayer

Dear Lord, in Your Word, we read about how You send angels to protect us. Help us believe Your Word and know those angels are near, even when we least expect it. *In Jesus' name, amen.*

COFFEE CHAT NOTES

28

DRAWING CLOSE TO GOD

"But it is good for me to draw near to God; I have put my trust in the Lord God, That I may declare all your works." (Psalm 73:28 NKJV)

THE LIFELONG DESIRE OF every Christian ought to be to draw closer to God. However, though we long to be more intimate with our Creator, we often don't know how to go about it. Drawing closer to God is often a moment-by-moment time of growth rather than a one-time event. One step at a time, we learn about His ways and His love for us when we read His Word, the Bible. This often leads us to a place of repentance, as sin in our lives is a stumbling block to our nearness to Him. Forgiving others who have wronged us is a requirement for being close to God.

Repentance and forgiveness are necessary in prayer as we seek to please our Lord. He is loving and gracious to forgive us as we forgive others.

This can and ought to be our way of life. It is not weighty or hard to do this, as He is our strength in weakness. God wants us to come to Him, and He will give us peace and a sense of closeness to Him that cannot be duplicated by any other means.

> "Draw near to God, and He will draw near to you. Cleanse your hands, you sinners; and purify your hearts, you double-minded."
> (James 4:8 NKJV)

Prayer

Dear God, we long for Your presence. Help us spend time with You daily as we pray and read Your Word. We believe You will draw near to us. *In Jesus' name, amen.*

COFFEE CHAT NOTES

29

FINDING OUR WAY HOME

"Surely your goodness and love will follow me all the
days of my life, and I will dwell in the house of the
Lord forever." (Psalm 23:6)

HOME SHOULD EVOKE FEELINGS of rest, relaxation, safety, acceptance, refuge, and belonging. We long for home! We dream of going home! We even get homesick!

Countless masses cannot say their home is a positive or nourishing place. Home is a space for them where strife, chaos, loneliness, and uncertainty reside. For others, there is no place to call home. Nowhere to get away from it all. They are a member of the homeless tribe!

With all our regrets, mistakes, missteps, and confusion on the journey, we still get to dwell in a place of *beloved* security, with or without an earthly home. We realize once and for all that we have always been *beloved,* no matter how *broken.* Now is the time to live out the remainder of life with that *beloved* identity! Jesus tells us He is preparing a Heavenly home for us. What a place of splendor that will be!

On this earth, we long for the perfect, idyllic home, often moving from place to place in pursuit of that dream. Maybe that is because we are searching for the perfect home that awaits us one day in Heaven. Whether we are homeless or live in the best mansion money can buy, this world is not our home but a temporary dwelling place. For those who believe in the Lord Jesus Christ for salvation, our perfect and final home will be Heaven with our Savior. All the uncertain and unfamiliar places in this earthly life will be no more. Peace, rest, and joy will be our reality. *We will be home at last.*

At ninety-two, my grandmother went to be with the Lord while in intensive care. The morning after her passing, I went to the hospital with my mother and two aunts. The attending nurses who had been with her throughout the night told us that as she grew closer to the end of her life, she sounded like a young girl. They could hear her words, spoken clearly and softly. "Oh, it is beautiful. I'll soon be home." We knew of her faith in Jesus and assurance of salvation, so those words comforted us.

To be a child of God with an assurance of salvation and a home in Heaven at the end of this life means we believe the Bible is God's infallible Word. We acknowledge that Jesus was born, died on the cross, was buried, and rose again to pay the penalty for our sins. When we repent for doing life our way and believe in Jesus and His promises, we will become a child of the One who loves us more than we can comprehend. I believe we will be at home in complete peace and purpose only in surrender to His love, promises, and plan.

"My Father's house has many rooms; if that were not so, would I have told you that I am going there to prepare a place for you? And if I go and prepare a place for you, I will come back and take you to be with me that you also may be where I am." (John 14:2–3)

Prayer

Dear God, we thank you for our earthly homes, knowing that many people are homeless. Please help them on their journey. Thank you for the blessed hope of being with You in Heaven, where our *forever home* awaits us. We are assured of a home in Heaven when we accept You as our personal Savior. *In Jesus' name, amen.*

COFFEE CHAT NOTES

30

ACCEPTING GOD'S LOVE

"But God demonstrates His own love toward us, in
that while we were still sinners, Christ died for us."
(Romans 5:8 NKJV)

WE MAY FIND IT hard to believe that God—the Creator of the universe, loves us. We feel small and insignificant compared to the vastness of all of creation. Sometimes, we conjure up reasons why God would not or could not love us. Maybe we have sinned too much, have not read the Bible, or attended church in a long time—perhaps never.

I taught a Sunday School class of nine-year-old girls. One Sunday, I shared a story with them: "Little Boat Twice Owned." It was the story of a father who helped his young son build a wooden boat that he could put out on the water and sail from the dock with a string attached to it, much like flying a kite. A storm came up one day, and the little boat was lost at sea. The father reasoned it would be too difficult to craft another as good as the first. Weeks later, still saddened by the loss of his prized boat, the boy went shopping with his father to see if they might find a similar boat to the one he lost.

As father and son went from store to store looking for a replacement boat, they saw it! The exact boat that once belonged to the son was in the store window for sale! They went into the store to inquire about the boat in the window. Once inside, they learned that the boat had washed up on shore a few miles away, and the store owner found it. After doing some repairs as it had been *broken*, he varnished it up to look new and put it in the window for sale. The father told how he had built that boat for his son and how it was lost. The store owner said he would have to sell it to them as he couldn't return it because of his restoration work. So, after paying for the boat, the father and son left the store. As the son walked away with both arms securely around his precious boat, he was heard saying: "You're mine twice—once because I made you, and twice because I bought you."

This heartfelt story speaks of God's immense love for us. God loves us because He first made us, then He bought us with the sacrifice of His one and only Son. He loves us not for who we are but because of who He is. He is the essence of love. He made us; we are the object of His mercy and grace. He loved us before we were ever thought of. He loved us when we were sinners and far from Him. We can't earn His love. We are not too *broken*, nor have we made too many mistakes, for Him to love us.

The Bible tells us in Psalm 139 how much He thinks of us. We are fearfully and wonderfully made (Psalm 139:14). We are one of a kind. He loves each of us as if we were the only ones He created. How marvelous is this precious Gospel! The Good News of this Gospel is found in His love letter to us—the Bible.

The story of God's love for us can be found throughout the Bible. However, a great place to start reading is in the book of John in the New Testament. *It is the most incredible story ever told.*

> "For I am convinced that neither death nor life, neither angels nor demons, neither the present nor the future, nor any powers, neither height nor depth nor anything else in all creation will be able to separate us from the love of God that is in Christ Jesus our Lord."
> (Romans 8:38)

Prayer

Dear God, we love You because You first loved us, died, and rose again for our salvation. Thank you for this wondrous love that cannot be found anywhere on this earth. *In Jesus' name, amen.*

Coffee Chat Notes

JESUS LOVES ME

ANNA B. WARNER, 1860

Jesus loves me—this I know, for the Bible tells me so.
Little ones to Him belong; they are weak, but He is strong.

Jesus loves me, He who died, Heaven's gates to open wide.
He will wash away my sin; let His little child come in.

Jesus loves me—loves me still, Though I'm very weak and ill.
From His shining throne on high comes to watch me where I lie.

Jesus loves me, He will stay close beside me all the way.
Then His little child will take up to Heaven for His dear sake.

Yes, Jesus loves me, yes, Jesus loves me,
yes, Jesus loves me, the Bible tells me so.

A Prayer for Salvation

If you desire to accept God's plan of salvation for your life and be in the right relationship with Him, you can express your feelings in a prayer to God.

Even though He already knows our hearts, He tells us in the Bible to pray to express our desires and needs. This prayer is only a suggested prayer. Your own words are perfectly acceptable to God when they are from your heart, spoken with sincerity and reverence.

Prayer

Jesus, I believe You are the Son of God. You died on the cross, You were buried, and You rose from the grave three days later to pay the penalty for my sin.

Please forgive me for trying to go my own way (without You). I repent and turn away from my sin. I believe in You and choose to live a life that pleases You.

I invite You to enter my life as my Savior and Lord. I want to follow You and learn about You by reading Your Word, the Bible.

Thank You for Your gift of eternal life and Your Holy Spirit, who now lives within me.

In Jesus' name, amen.

"Once, we were lost, *broken*, and without hope. Now we have been found, and having turned from our sinful nature, we know beyond a shadow of a doubt that we are His *beloved* now and for all eternity. Having been reconciled to Him, we have hope and assurance that we will see Jesus and our loved ones who have gone before."

Thank You To...

My writing friends: **Berni**, **Catherine**, **Corina**, **Denise**, **Kathryn**, and **Melodie**. We met in mid-2020 as members of the online writing group *Writing the Waves*. I have appreciated learning with you, and your support was priceless in contributing to the beginning stages of my writing. Through all the tears and laughs, I desired to be a better writer because of your genuine friendship.

Andrea Lende, I would not have been able to complete this book without your vast knowledge of publishing. You inspired me with your positivity, can-do attitude, and keen insights.

Ruth Hovsepian, I appreciate your expertise in all things publishing. The value you have brought to this process has been exceptional and professional.

Finally, yet always first, **Jesus**, my Savior, for never abandoning me. You have always loved and helped me, giving me hope whenever all hope seemed lost. I am grateful for Your love, mercy, and grace. I treasure Your presence and provision and trust Your promises.

SCRIPTURE REFERENCES

Ruth 1:16–17 NKJV
John 3:16
Psalm 139:14–18

Day 1 – Psalm 27:14, Romans 12:12
Day 2 – Jeremiah 18:1–6 NLT, Isaiah 64:8
Day 3 – Psalm 38:4, 21–22, Philippians 4:6 NLT
Day 4 – Psalm 1:6 NLT, Proverbs 16:17 NLT
Day 5- 2 Corinthians 10:5, 2 Corinthians 7:10
Day 6 – Joshua 1:9, Galatians 6:4
Day 7 – Isaiah 53:5, 1 Peter 2:24 NLT
Day 8 – Ephesians 4:2 NLT, Proverbs 4:7 NLT
Day 9 – Proverbs 4:25–27 NLT, Psalm 42:1 NLT
Day 10 – Proverbs 24:16, Psalm 147:3 NLT
Day 11 – Proverbs 13:12 NLT, Psalms 37:4
Day 12 – Matthew 10:31 NLT, Isaiah 61:7
Day 13 – Psalm 118:24 NKJV, Proverbs 17:22
Day 14 – John 15:4–8, Jeremiah 17:7–8
Day 15 – Isaiah 26:3 NLT, Philippians 4:8 NLT

SCRIPTURE REFERENCES 117

Day 16 – Philippians 3:13–14, Galatians 6:9

Day 17 – Romans 15:13, John 14:27

Day 18 – Proverbs 3:5–6, Psalm 56:3

Day 19 – 1 Peter 5:10, Romans 8:28

Day 20 – Psalm 119:105 NLT, John 1:5 NLT

Day 21 – Psalm 27:1, John 3:21 NLT

Day 22 – John 1:10–11, Isaiah 53:3

Day 23 – Psalm 23, Isaiah 53:6 NLT

Day 24 – Proverbs 4:23 NLT, Psalm 139:23–24 NLT

Day 25 – Romans 5:5 NLT, Psalm 34:18

Day 26 – Psalm 23:4 NLT, Jeremiah 29:11 NKJV

Day 27 – Psalm 91:11, Hebrews 1:14

Day 28 – Psalm 73: 28 NKJV, James 4:8 NKJV

Day 29 – Psalm 23:6, John 14:2–3

Day 30 – Romans 5:8 NKJV, Romans 8:38

ABOUT THE AUTHOR

Patricia J. Doucet is committed to encouraging women to pursue their God-given aspirations regardless of detours, obstacles, and setbacks. She is empathetic to women in their struggles and shares her experiences with clarity, compassion, and humor to inspire them to overcome and find wholeness. Her ministry, *From Broken to Beloved*, helps women take the next steps toward restoration and peace with courage and conviction.

Patricia graduated from Master's College and Seminary in Ontario, Canada, and has served in various ministry roles throughout her life. These days, she connects with those she encourages through virtual *Coffee Chats,* blog posts, podcast appearances, and inspirational messages. She lives with her chef-musician husband in Nova Scotia and has two sons, a daughter, and a son-in-law, all of whom she cherishes.

Starting her day with a freshly brewed cup of coffee is a morning priority. She enjoys reading, walking, interior decorating, landscape painting, fashion, engaging in sincere and uplifting conversations, playing the piano, and taking scenic road trips. Spending quality time with her loved ones is important to her, and she strongly believes in the value of authentic and honest relationships.

Patricia's journey of resilience and perseverance is a testament to God's faithfulness, grace, mercy, and love.

WAYS TO CONNECT WITH PATRICIA

Website: www.patriciajdoucet.com
Email: pat@patriciajdoucet.com
Instagram & Facebook: @patriciajdoucet
YouTube: @PatriciaJDoucet

If you have been blessed by reading this devotional, please consider leaving a review on Amazon. Your review will help more women find and be encouraged by this book. Thank you so much!

www.ingramcontent.com/pod-product-compliance
Lightning Source LLC
Chambersburg PA
CBHW070201100426
42743CB00013B/2997